healing with
crystals

A concise guide to using

crystals for health, harmony

and happiness

D1342240

Simon Lilly

HERMES
HOUSE

The edition published by Hermes House

© Anness Publishing Limited 2002 updated 2003..

Hermes House is an imprint of Anness Publishing Limited,
Hermes House, 88–89 Blackfriars Road, London SE1 8HA

Publisher: Joanna Lorenz
Production Controller: Joanna King

Publisher's Note:
The Reader should not regard the recommendations, ideas and techniques
expressed and described in this book as substitutes for the advice of a
qualified medical practitioner or other qualified professional.
Any use to which the recommendations, ideas and techniques
are put is at the reader's sole discretion and risk.

Printed in Hong Kong/China

3 5 7 9 10 8 6 4

contents

introduction

Crystals can be found in every part of the world in many shapes and forms. They are symbols of wealth and power, as in the gems on a crown, and certain stones have been prized for millennia by healers, shamans and priests for their curative powers.

The ancient traditions of crystal healing are undergoing a revival in modern times, and many people find crystals bring them real benefits and lasting changes. This book introduces you to safe and easy techniques of crystal healing that you can try in your home and office. It is also an invitation to discover for yourself the subtle and mysterious power of healing crystals.

How a crystal is born

Our word "crystal" is derived from the ancient Greek term "krystallos", meaning "ice". The Greeks thought rock crystal was water that had frozen so completely that it could never melt again.

The Greeks were not entirely mistaken, of course, because ice is indeed the crystal form of water, and we call ice crystals snowflakes, and recognize their six-sided forms. Every substance, from water to carbon, or blood, will form crystalline structures given the correct circumstances of temperature and pressure.

▲ THE INTERNAL LATTICE STRUCTURE OF A CRYSTAL IS REVEALED IN ITS EXTERNAL GEOMETRY OF FLAT PLANES AND ANGLES.

Deep within the Earth's crust superheated gases and mineral-rich solutions find their way towards the surface along cracks and fissures at very high temperatures. As they cool, the atoms of the boiling gases and liquids begin to arrange themselves in regular patterns. These repeating three-dimensional patterns of atoms are known as crystal lattices. All crystals have their own characteristic microscopic lattice forms.

As the mineral solutions near the Earth's surface cool and the pressure drops, atoms from different minerals often combine to create more complex crystals. Usually harder minerals, such as diamond, emerald and quartz, form at a higher pressure and temperature, and have a dense lattice structure. Softer minerals, such as calcite and turquoise crystallize at lower temperatures and have a more open lattice.

The structure of the Earth is continually changing, but the essential quality of all crystals is their very stable atomic structure. Whatever the outside force – whether heat, pressure, electricity or light – crystals always make minute adjustments to restore their internal stability and lattice form.

This unique orderliness and stability makes crystals valuable in modern technology. They are used in watches and lasers, and as switching and regulating devices in engines powering all manner of things from cars to space shuttles.

No one is really certain how crystals help in healing, but it may be that the very nature of crystals increases the levels of harmony in their immediate environment. Crystals are known to be the most orderly matter in the universe. Because coherence is a stronger natural force than chaos, introducing order into a disorganized state – for example, by placing a crystal on an aching muscle – can increase the chances of the imbalance or disharmony returning to stability and order.

Whether the imbalance in us is a physical illness or emotional or mental upset, our energy pattern has lost its order. The simple, powerful resonance of a crystal, with its locked-in power of ancient fire and unique purity of form, may help us reinstate our own balance and harmony.

▼ WHETHER NATURAL OR CARVED, THE INTERNAL ORDERLINESS OF A CRYSTAL'S ATOMS CAN INFLUENCE ITS SURROUNDINGS.

Crystal variations

Crystals come in all manner of colours, shapes and sizes. They consist of many different ingredients, determined by conditions, such as location, temperature and pressure. Here are some of their many types and forms.

GEODE

If a mineral solution crystallizes in a hollow rock cavity, and the rock then erodes, geode crystals are formed. Geodes can be of many shapes and colours, according to the type of original rock and minerals.

PHANTOM CRYSTAL

These stones are so named because within the body of a phantom are smaller outlines of the crystal form. During formation, where a crystal stops growing and then begins again, a few particles of other minerals may settle on the faces, clearly showing the stages of growth. These are fascinating and beautiful crystals to look at and make good personal meditation crystals.

FLUORITE CRYSTAL

This gemstone forms around a cubic lattice structure making interlocking cubes, octahedral and pyramid crystals. It comes in a wide variety of colours, though violet is one of the commonest.

CELESTITE

This is soft stone, which is most often formed by the evaporation of water from mineral deposits, leaving a clear and delicate blue crystal.

AMETRINE

As the name suggests, this is a mix of amethyst, giving the violet colour, and citrine, which adds the golden yellow. Both are varieties of the common mineral, quartz.

ROCK CRYSTAL WANDS

Crystals can be microscopic in size or very large indeed, growing to several metres in length. Long, thin prisms of crystal can be effective healing tools.

RUTILATED QUARTZ

A clear or smoky crystal, rutilated quartz contains fine threads of golden or orange rutile (titanium oxide) crystals.

IRON PYRITES

This ore of iron and sulphur is a common mineral in the Earth's crust. It can form perfect single cubes, sparkly masses resembling gold and flat, disc-like clusters of crystal.

AMETHYST

This is another form of quartz, whose purple or violet colour comes from iron particles in the crystal.

CITRINE

A form of quartz that occurs when violet amethyst is subjected to heat, either naturally or artificially.

BLUE LACE AGATE

From the chalcedony family of crystals blue lace agate is made up of tiny blue and white quartz crystals, in swirls or lines.

OPAL

Is a member of the quartz family with a high water content, creating the colourful play of light. It is microcrystalline with no regular geometry visible.

AMBER

A fossil pine tree resin, amber is found in rich yellows, orange brown and deep reds and greens, often with trapped foliage or even insects embedded within.

The chakra system

Knowledge of the chakra system comes from ancient Indian texts. These describe energy centres or chakras in the body, with seven major points arranged along the spinal column. These chakras are used in crystal healing.

THE SEVEN CHAKRAS

In Indian philosophy the chakras are the areas of energy near the spine where particular internal organs and systems are focused. Seven points are counted along the spinal column from the crown of the head down to the bottom of the spine. Each chakra is associated with a particular physical function and also a mental or emotional state; each has come to be represented by a particular colour. By combining the appropriate crystals with the chakra centres it is possible to help restore natural functioning of the body at many different levels.

▲ COLOUR AND POSITION OF EACH OF THE CHAKRAS.

CHAKRA FUNCTIONS

• the first or base chakra at the base of the spine is red in colour, and concerns physical survival, and energy distribution in the body;

• the second or sacral chakra, apart from its control of the reproductive system, is concerned with creativity and pleasure-seeking; its colour is orange;

• the third or solar plexus chakra, is located between the bottom of the ribcage and the navel. Yellow in colour, it connects with confidence, personal power and gut instinct;

• the fourth or heart chakra is at the centre of the chest, is green and deals with relationships and personal development;

• the fifth or throat chakra controls the power of speech and communication, including learning, and is a blue colour;

• the sixth, third eye or brow chakra is in the centre of the forehead, its colour is indigo and it supervises mental powers, memory and psychic abilities;

• the seventh or crown chakra is located at the top of the head, its colour is violet, and it oversees the balance of the chakra system and higher spiritual growth.

THE SUBTLE BODIES

The fact that we consist of more than the physical body is apparent to many people, even if science so far fails to confirm it. We all have felt somebody intruding into our personal space or sensed the presence of others.

Some people can discern auras around our physical body, and almost anyone can be taught to sense the different qualities within a person's auric field. Like the chakras, each level of the subtle bodies represents a certain frequency of personal energy.

The Indian philosophers and yogis of old described complex patterns in our "subtle bodies", and identified different energy systems beyond the physical:
• the etheric body is closest to the physical and provides the blueprint for the body and its organs. A disruption of harmony within the etheric almost always precedes physical illness;
• the emotional body contains our ever-changing patterns of emotions and feelings. Being the least stable of the subtle bodies, it is the easiest one to modify with crystals;
• the mental body contains the patterns in which we have organized our understanding of reality, with our beliefs and ideas, and everyday thinking;
• the finer subtle bodies are concerned with our spiritual identity and our connection with the universal or collective unconscious, as Carl Jung called it. These levels can also be effectively balanced by crystal healing techniques, though it is less easy to define these subtle areas of life.

▶ THE SUBTLE BODIES ARE THE FINE, NON-PHYSICAL LEVELS OF OUR BEING.

Crystal colours

The simplest methods of crystal healing combine the colour of stones with the appropriate chakra. The colour of a crystal will always indicate its main energy function, so it is useful to learn the basic properties of each colour.

RED (BASE CHAKRA)

This colour stimulates, activates and energizes, but also grounds and focuses. Associated crystals are garnet, jasper and ruby.

GARNET

ORANGE (SACRAL CHAKRA)

A mix of red and yellow, orange combines their activating and organizing roles in boosting energy flows or treating blockages. Related crystals include dark citrine, orange calcite, carnelian, topaz and copper.

ORANGE CALCITE

YELLOW (SOLAR PLEXUS)

The vibrant colour yellow is concerned with strengthening and preserving the body's systems (e.g. nervous, digestive and

AMBER

immune). The associated crystals are amber, rutilated quartz, tiger's eye, citrine quartz and iron pyrites.

GREEN (HEART CHAKRA)

As the mid-spectrum colour, green acts to balance our emotions and relationships, encouraging growth in all areas of life.

MALACHITE

Heart stones include bloodstone, green aventurine, malachite, amazonite, moss agate, peridot and emerald.

BLUE (THROAT CHAKRA)

The blue chakra relates principally to communication, both within ourselves and from us to the outside world. Related stones are celestite, blue lace agate, turquoise and aquamarine.

AQUAMARINE

LAPIS LAZULI

INDIGO
(BROW CHAKRA)

Dark blue, or indigo, governs perception, understanding and intuition. Associated with this centre are lapis lazuli, sodalite, kyanite, azurite and sapphire.

VIOLET (CROWN CHAKRA)

The traditional colour of spiritual illumination and service, violet also represents the mind's control of the body and the self. Related stones include amethyst, fluorite, sugilite and iolite.

AMETHYST

WHITE

With qualities of universality and clarity, white is also connected to the crown chakra. White light contains and reflects all other colours, symbolizing the potential to cleanse or purify energy. Clear quartz, herkimer diamond, Iceland spa, moonstone and selenite are favoured white crystals.

MOONSTONE

TOURMALINE

BLACK

The colour black absorbs light as much as white reflects it. Black reveals the hidden potential of a person or condition. It holds its energies in reserve, grounds and anchors energy. Related crystals are smoky quartz, obsidian, tourmaline and haematite.

ROSE QUARTZ

PINK

A blend of both red and white, pink is associated with the base and heart chakras, and works to restore underlying balance. Pink stones include rose quartz, rhodonite and rhodocrosite.

MULTICOLOURED

These are various, and their actions reflect their colour combinations. Rainbow inclusions can be found in many transparent crystals including quartz. Other stones are azurite-malachite, hawk's eye, opal, labradorite and ametrine.

AMETRINE

Choosing and cleansing crystals

All the crystals described in this book are relatively easy to find at a reasonable price. When building up a personal collection, aim for quality rather than quantity. Purchase stones that attract you and that you feel happy with.

CHOOSING YOUR CRYSTALS

When selecting suitable crystals, remember that you will be placing stones on a relaxed, prone body, whether yours or somebody else's. So avoid stones that are too heavy or too small. Flatter stones stay in place better than round ones. Try to acquire at least two stones per spectrum colour.

Small natural crystals of clear quartz are often needed, so try to find about a dozen, each of around 2–3 cm (¾–1¼ in) in length. Small crystals of smoky quartz, amethyst and citrine have many uses.

A small, hand-sized crystal cluster of clear quartz or amethyst is useful for cleansing and charging your stones.

Larger single stones and tumbled stones are good to hold and as meditation aids.

▾ HANDLE YOUR CRYSTALS CAREFULLY, SINCE SOME ARE SOFT AND CAN SCRATCH, WHILE OTHERS ARE HARD AND BRITTLE.

CLEANSING YOUR CRYSTALS

New stones should be cleansed before you begin using them. Cleansing removes unwanted energy from the crystals and restores them to their original clarity. Cleanse your crystals every time you use them for healing. Try the following methods:

• Sun and water: hold the stones under running water for a minute and place them in the sun to dry.

• Incense or smudge stick: hold the crystal within the smoke; herbs such as sandalwood, sage, cedar and frankincense are good purifiers.

• Sound: the vibrations of a bell, gong or tuning fork can energetically clean a crystal.

• Sea salt: put dry sea salt (avoid salt water as it can corrode crystals)

▲ MATERIALS FOR CLEANSING CRYSTALS INCLUDE SALT, WATER, A TUNING FORK, INCENSE AND SMUDGE STICKS.

in a small container and bury your crystal in the salt crystals for approximately 24 hours.

▼ CLEAN STONES ON A CRYSTAL CLUSTER (BELOW LEFT) OR SURROUND ONE STONE WITH CLEAR QUARTZ POINTS FOR 24 HOURS (BELOW).

Techniques: know your stones

When you acquire a new crystal, spend some time getting familiar with it and developing a sensitivity to its subtle energy field. Try these simple techniques, being aware of how you feel at each step.

SENSING YOUR CRYSTALS

1 Examine your crystal from all angles, then close your eyes and feel it as you hold it in your hands for a minute or two.

2 Open your eyes and gaze at the crystal. Then close your eyes once more. Does the crystal feel the same as before?

3 Hold the crystal in one hand, then the other. Also try holding it in both hands.

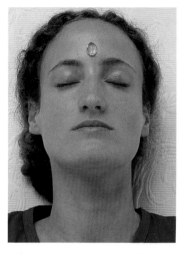

▲ LIE DOWN, CLOSE YOUR EYES AND RELAX AND SENSE THE EFFECT OF YOUR CHOSEN CRYSTAL ON A CHAKRA POINT.

4 Now lie back and place the crystal on your chakra centres. The solar plexus, heart and brow are often good places to try.

5 Still lying down, place the crystal close to your body, noting how it feels on the right and left sides, near your head and feet.

◄ DEVELOP A SENSITIVITY TO A NEW CRYSTAL BY HOLDING IT.

A VISUALIZATION EXERCISE

This exercise is best done with a crystal you already know and feel comfortable with.

1 Sit comfortably and hold the crystal in both hands. Relax and focus on it.

2 Slowly let your awareness float down into the crystal and come to rest there.

3 Think how the crystal feels – warm or damp, cool or dry, smooth or rough? Take a minute or two to explore its inner energy.

4 Relax again, and attune yourself to the crystal's inner vibration or sound – is it a tone, a pulse or a tune, high or low, simple or complex? Listen for a few minutes, then relax again.

5 Take some deep breaths, then imagine you are breathing in the crystal's energy. Does it have a taste or smell?

6 Relax again, and open your inner eyes to imagine the lattice structure of the crystal, its inner light and landscape. Don't analyze anything you see, just let it come and go.

7 Now become aware again of the crystal's taste, smell, sounds and touch. Gradually bring your awareness out of the crystal and back into your own body. Make notes so that you will be able to remember your experiences better.

▼ HOLD THE CRYSTAL NEAR YOUR SOLAR PLEXUS AND IMAGINE YOUR BREATH IS ENTERING YOUR BODY THROUGH THE STONE.

Meditating with crystals

Clear quartz can be a wonderful aid to meditation and contemplation. Just think, you are looking into solid matter of extraordinary stability and subtlety. Its constant harmony may help you increase or regain your own.

If you are upset or stressed, gaze deeply into your favourite quartz crystal, and allow your mind to quieten down. When the body and mind begins to settle, it is easier to find solutions and balance.

Sit quietly with your quartz crystal and look closely at it. Then relax and shut your eyes. Pay attention to how you feel and think. Are your thoughts calm or busy, happy or sad? Note any sensations in your body.

After a few minutes, repeat the process using other quartz crystals and compare your experiences. Take deep, slow, breaths before you get up.

▲ Sit in a comfortable position to meditate with your crystals.

Sit comfortably with a smoky quartz in your left hand and a clear quartz in your right. After a few moments swap them around. Do you feel any difference? Once you find a combination that suits you, try to spend a few minutes every day, preferably at the same time, sitting and meditating with your favourite crystals.

◄ Gaze into the depths of your crystal and close your eyes.

ACTIVE CONTEMPLATION

In another form of crystal meditation, place the crystal in a position in front of you that lets you gaze into its depths. Don't try to control your thoughts or worry about "doing it right". Just relax and enjoy the stone's company. Then close your eyes, feel calm, take some deep breaths and follow your thoughts. Open or close your eyes as you wish, but take the crystal's energy with you as you meditate.

If you find it difficult to relax and meditate with one crystal, you can make a pattern or mandala with your stones. This "active contemplation" may suit you better.

▾ MAKING A PATTERN OR A MANDALA OF YOUR STONES CAN CALM AN AGITATED MIND.

Hand-held crystal healing

We are all aware that positive thoughts are healing and negative thoughts are harmful. Using a quartz crystal in combination with directed positive thought can release a flow of healing energy, towards ourselves or to others.

A quartz crystal will direct the energy either towards or away from your body, depending on where the point is facing. An additional crystal can be held in the "absorbing" or "receiving" hand. This helps us to feel the quartz's healing energy clearly in our awareness.

ENERGY CHANNELLING

If you have an area of over-excited energy, you may feel congested, hot, tense, irritated or frustrated. Place the palm of your left hand over that area. Hold the quartz crystal in your right hand, with its point away from you and towards the ground. Breathe deeply and evenly, imagining all the excess energy releasing from your body. Let it pass out through the crystal into the earth and away from you.

If you need to recharge depleted energy or want extra healing energy, the process is reversed. Hold the quartz in your right hand, pointing it towards the area concerned. Hold your left hand away from your body, with the palm facing upwards. Breathe deeply and evenly, imagining healing energies from the universe passing from your upturned hand, through the crystal and into you.

▸ TO RELEASE EXCESS ENERGY INTO THE EARTH HOLD A QUARTZ CRYSTAL IN YOUR RIGHT HAND POINTING AWAY FROM YOU AND TOWARDS THE GROUND.

1 To clear away unwanted energy, release tensions and help relaxation, hold your "receiving" hand close to your partner. With your "directing" hand, hold the quartz and allow the excess energy to drain away into the earth. Try moving the quartz in circles to aid the process.

2 When you finish, revitalize the other person's aura by holding the crystal in the "directing" hand, with the point towards the body. Hold the "receiving" hand palm upwards and allow the universal energy to flow through the crystal into the newly cleansed area or chakra.

Try these exercises with opposite hands to see how it feels. Right-handed people often find their left hand more absorbing or "receiving", and the right hand directs the outward flow of energy. Left-handed people may find the opposite is true for them.

Grounding and centring

When you feel solidly anchored in the present, with a sense of inner calm and clarity, that is the experience of being grounded. Being ungrounded is a state of feeling confused and unfocused.

GETTING GROUNDED

▲ ADOPT THIS LAYOUT TO CENTRE AND GROUND YOUR ENERGIES IN JUST A COUPLE OF MINUTES.

Holding a grounding stone can help us focus chaotic energy and restore everyday awareness. A simple grounding exercise is to sit or stand with your feet firmly on the floor, then imagine roots growing from your feet into the earth. With each breath, allow the roots to spread deeper and wider until you feel anchored and secure.

A GROUNDING LAYOUT

Lie down on your back and relax. Place one smoky quartz crystal point downwards at the base of the throat and another between the legs or close to the base of the spine. In most crystal healing patterns it helps to use a grounding stone close to the base chakra or between the feet and legs. Any changes created by the healing can then be more easily integrated into daily life.

▲ MANY OF THE CRYSTALS THAT HELP IN GROUNDING ARE DARK OR RED. TOP, LEFT TO RIGHT: SNOWFLAKE OBSIDIAN, HAEMATITE, DARK TOURMALINE, SMOKY QUARTZ, ONYX. BOTTOM, LEFT TO RIGHT: STAUROLITE, CITRINE, JASPER.

CENTRING YOURSELF

Feeling centred means being in a state of mental, emotional and physical balance. You know your boundaries and feel in control of your energies. Centring can be achieved by techniques that focus your attention within your body.

1 Sit quietly, and be aware of your breathing. Feel yourself breathing in from your feet and back out through your feet into the earth.

2 Be aware of your midline — an imaginary line extending from above the top of your head to below your feet, situated just in

▲ RESTORE YOUR FOCUS WITH A BLACK GROUNDING STONE.

front of your spine. Pull your breath into this midline from above and breathe out through the line into the ground. Repeat until you feel calm and focused.

3 Strike a bell, gong or tuning fork, and listen for as long as the sound remains.

4 Slowly and consciously bring your fingertips together and hold them for a minute or two. Take deep breaths in.

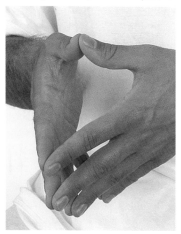

▲ BRING YOUR FINGERTIPS TOGETHER SLOWLY TO FOCUS YOUR ATTENTION.

Pendulum healing

Many people will be familiar with the idea of using a pendulum for dowsing. A pendulum made from a natural crystal can, however, be used as a healing tool in its own right, even if the individual has no experience with dowsing.

Using a crystal pendulum for healing is effective in removing energy imbalances from the body's finer energy sytems.

▲ THERE ARE MANY STYLES OF PENDULUM, SO CHOOSE ONE THAT FEELS RIGHT FOR YOU.

The healer has a clear intent that the pendulum will only move away from a neutral swing (back and forth) when it finds an energy imbalance that can be corrected quickly and safely. The crystal will move in a pattern that allows the imbalance to be cleared and will then return to the neutral swing. It is not necessary to know the nature of the imbalances – they may be on many levels from the physical, emotional, mental or spiritual bodies. Nor does the physical location of an imbalance necessarily indicate that it is where the source of a problem lies. The movement of a crystal's energy field through the aura simply helps to break up any build-up of unhelpful patterns, and releases them safely.

Whilst dowsing for assessment, any sort of pendulum, wood, metal, plastic, glass or stone can be used. Healing techniques using pendulums, however, will best employ a natural crystal. Because every crystal has its own range of properties the best crystal pendulums to use are ones that have a broad, generalized energy. These will respond to and balance many different types of energy imbalance. Clear quartz, amethyst and smoky quartz all make useful healing pendulums. Other clear and transparent crystals also work with broad ranges of energy.

As it is a healing tool, a crystal pendulum needs to be cleansed regularly before and after use.

REMOVING ENERGY IMBALANCES

▲ HOLD THE PENDULUM LIGHTLY AND FIRMLY BETWEEN THE THUMB AND FOREFINGER.

1 Grip the pendulum. Allow the wrist to relax and hold your arm in a comfortable position.

2 Start the pendulum moving in a line, to and fro, in what is known as a neutral swing.

3 Slowly move up the centre of the body, beginning beneath the feet. Wherever the pendulum swings away from the neutral, simply stay at that point until the neutral swing returns.

4 When you reach the top of the head, go back to the feet and begin again. Now hold the pendulum nearer to one side of the body and again slowly move upwards. Repeat for the other side.

5 If the pendulum goes on moving over an imbalance for a long time, put another crystal on that spot and move on. Later check the area again. An appropriate choice of stone will have balanced the energies so that the pendulum remains in a neutral swing.

Although some methods place importance on the way a pendulum moves, in this technique any movement away from neutral simply indicates an imbalance that the crystal is able to correct.

▲ CRYSTAL PENDULUMS CAN HELP TO BALANCE THE SUBTLE BODIES.

Balancing the chakras

One of the easiest ways to balance the chakra system is to place a stone of the appropriate colour on each area. This will give each chakra a boost of its own vibration without altering its energies or the system's overall harmony.

SEVEN COLOUR CHAKRA LAYOUT

For this exercise use small stones, such as polished or tumbled crystals. Make sure that they have been energetically cleansed before beginning. If working on yourself, lay the stones near to where you will be lying so that they are easy to find and position. Even though you might sense little change, allow yourself a few moments to recover after having the stones in place for five or six minutes.

1 It is a helpful start to place a grounding stone, such as smoky quartz, between your legs to act as an anchor.

2 For the base chakra, place a red stone at the bottom of the spine or two stones of the same sort at the top of each leg.

3 For the second or sacral chakra, position an orange-coloured stone on the lower abdomen.

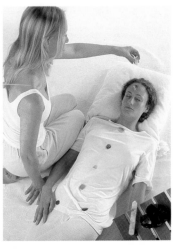

▲ REST THE CROWN CHAKRA STONE AT THE TOP OF THE HEAD. CHOOSE CLEAR QUARTZ IF YOU HAVE USED AN AMETHYST FOR THE BROW.

4 At the solar plexus use a yellow stone, positioned between the navel and ribcage. If there is tension here, put an energy-shifting stone, such as tiger's eye or clear quartz, on the diaphragm.

5 Place a green stone in the centre of the chest to balance the heart chakra. Add a pink stone for emotional clearing.

6 For the throat chakra use a light blue stone, placing it near the base of the throat, at the top of the breastbone.

7 An indigo or dark blue stone positioned in the centre of the forehead is used to balance the brow or third eye chakra. Amethyst or another purple stone may also be tried.

8 The crystal for the crown chakra should rest just above the top of your partner's head. If you choose an amethyst for the brow chakra, use a clear quartz crystal for the crown; if you used a dark blue stone for the brow, choose a violet crystal or gemstone to position at the crown chakra. It is always important to cleanse your stones at the end of a treatment.

INTUITIVE HEALING LAYOUTS

Once you become more confident in crystal healing or know the energies of the person you are treating better, allow yourself to be more intuitive in choosing suitable crystals for them.

1 Lay your crystals on the table. Then, after grounding your energies for a minute or two, and with the person's needs in mind, pick up the stones that attract your attention. Don't think of colours or even of chakras.

2 Place the stones where you feel they need to be on the body. Ask your partner how they feel, and make adjustments accordingly. After about five minutes remove the crystals and ground the energies with a smoky quartz.

▲ WHEN POSITIONING YOUR CHOSEN STONES TRY TO DO SO QUICKLY AND WITHOUT THINKING TOO HARD ABOUT IT.

balancing the chakras **27**

The crown chakra

Located just above the top of the head, the crown chakra has a violet and purple colour or aura. It supervises and balances the chakra system as a whole and channels universal life energy into the system.

Healing at this chakra will have an energizing effect on the whole body, though the effects may be slow to appear, because this most subtle of chakras works to clarify and harmonize the whole system. The crown chakra maintains our links to the rest of creation, feeding us much as the base chakra does.

Imbalances at the crown chakra can take the form of apathy and indifference, narrow-mindedness, loneliness

This is the centre at which imagination, inspiration, empathy and selfless service to others are nourished. Its colour is violet and purple, vestments of which are frequently chosen by secular and religious leaders to remind others of their power and authority. White, gold and magenta also relate to the crown chakra.

▸ TRY USING A CRYSTAL APPROPRIATE
FOR THE CROWN CHAKRA DURING TIMES OF
SELF-DOUBT, STRESS OR PROLONGED APATHY.

and lack of faith or belief. Sleep problems, stress and problems associated with learning may also be encountered.

CRYSTALS FOR THE CROWN CHAKRA
• AMETHYST is perhaps the most useful all-purpose stone used by crystal healers, and is especially popular as an aid to meditation. Amethyst acts to quieten the mind and will allow finer perceptions to manifest within us.

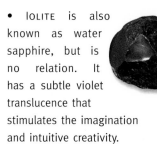

• FLUORITE exists in a variety of colours, often in the violet range, and it helps integrate subtle energies with normal consciousness, as well as aiding co-ordination, both physical and mental.

• SUGILITE can be useful in group situations, bringing greater collective harmony and coherence, and assisting those who dislike their circumstances and feel that they don't fit in.

• IOLITE is also known as water sapphire, but is no relation. It has a subtle violet translucence that stimulates the imagination and intuitive creativity.

• KUNZITE is pale pink and violet with a striated crystalline structure, and is good at removing emotional debris and helping in self-expression.

• CHAROITE AND ROCK CRYSTAL can also be used at the crown centre.

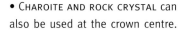

The brow chakra

The sixth chakra is located below the centre of the forehead, just above and between the brows and is our "inner eye". Its colour is indigo and, like the crown chakra, has been linked with both the pineal and pituitary glands.

This chakra is often referred to as the third eye, the single eye that looks deep within to see and understand as contrasted with the two physical eyes, which look outwards and receive optical data from the world of the senses.

The brow chakra is the "inner eye" of the imagination, creativity and dreaming. It "sees" hidden patterns and groups and grasps spiritual essences. This is a psychic place at the threshold of the inner and outer worlds, and is a natural seat of knowledge. It is no accident that when we think hard we often put our hand to this point to make our focus deeper.

Healing at this chakra can benefit many conditions linked to headaches and migraines, recurrent nightmares and bad sleep, depression and stress. The eyes, nose and ears can also gain much from treatments here, with eye strain, clogged sinuses and earache being eased with a

▸ TO CLEAR A BLOCKED NOSE MASSAGE BETWEEN THE BROWS WITH LEPIDOLITE.

gentle application of an amethyst, purple fluorite or lapis lazuli. Poor concentration and memory can also be improved by using these stones regularly.

CRYSTALS FOR THE BROW CHAKRA

Indigo or midnight blue is the colour of the third eye chakra, and among the stones which have been found to work best are:

• LAPIS LAZULI is a rock of different minerals that can stimulate the rapid release of stresses and energize the mind.

• SAPPHIRE, which can relax and bring peace to the mind and balance all aspects of the self by releasing tension.

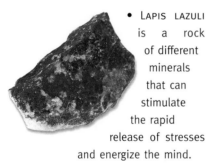

• SODALITE is similar to but less vivid a blue than lapis lazuli, and works to calm and open the mind to receiving new information and messages.

• KYANITE has a "fan-like" appearance and is favoured for moving on blocked energies and rapidly restoring the body's basic equilibrium.

• AZURITE also helps to unblock channels of communication and stimulate memory and recall.

• LEPIDOLITE and PURPLE FLUORITE are also often used to good effect at this centre.

The throat chakra

The throat chakra is concerned with the free flow of communication at all levels. It allows self-expression and personal creativity, enabling us to hear, learn and teach. Its colour and related crystals are light blue.

On the physical level this chakra governs the proper functioning of the throat area, which under stress can mean conditions such as tight shoulders, tonsillitis, laryngitis or sore throats. Crystals can help lighten these blockages.

More generally this is the centre of self-expression, which often reflects our self-image. Any difficulty in communicating, whether caused by emotional or physical problems, can be eased by balancing the energies of the throat chakra. Attention given to this chakra may be of considerable value.

Unblocking the subtle energies at the throat centre will allow us to say our piece and be heard. Emotions can also become blocked here as desires rise from the heart chakra and are unable to be expressed because of external restrictions, such as social values and family expectations. Working at this chakra can allow creativity to flow again.

▶ THROAT COMPLAINTS CAN BE TREATED BY WORKING THIS CHAKRA.

When stressed, we can often feel pressure on our neck and shoulders. A light blue crystal placed near the throat can quickly alleviate symptoms. This centre can often feel restricted in a healing session as stress is released. An appropriate stone will help to ease the flow and promote a relaxed sense of peace and openness.

CRYSTALS FOR THE THROAT CHAKRA
•TURQUOISE has been valued since ancient times as a supportive and protective stone, which can strengthen the subtle bodies and the fine communication systems within the body.

• BLUE LACE AGATE is a banded form of blue quartz that will calm and soothe, while at the same time lighten our thoughts.

• CELESTITE forms a delicate blue crystal that is "dreamy" in quality. It helps to lift heavy moods and to express spiritual needs. It is also useful for throat problems.

• AQUAMARINE is a blue variety of beryl and a stimulator of the body's own healing systems; it also supports efforts to stand our ground and be honest with our feelings.

• SAPPHIRE and SODALITE, also used for the brow chakra, can be valuable alternative crystals to try out at the throat centre.

The heart chakra

Located midway in the chakra system, the heart centre is associated with the colour green – the middle of the spectrum of light. The heart chakra is thus a place of balance, harmony and equilibrium at all levels.

have seriously life-damaging effects on the majority of animals, including humans. Restriction, even if it is only imaginary, depletes the immune system allowing disease and illness to take hold. Balancing the energies of the heart chakra can quickly restore life-energy throughout the body, creating a sense of calm, relaxation and the confidence to be able to make positive changes. Love is the open, expansive expression of the heart chakra when balanced.

The heart is nowadays associated with the emotions, but in the past it was thought to be the seat of the mind and the soul. This chakra balances our internal reality with the outside world, so is concerned with relationships of all kinds, especially how personal desires and growth can find an outlet via interactions with others.

Feelings of being trapped, the inability to escape from life circumstances and a loss of hope

▲ BALANCING THE HEART CHAKRA WILL HELP TO RESOLVE EMOTIONAL ISSUES AND CLARIFY DIRECTION IN LIFE.

CRYSTALS FOR THE HEART CHAKRA

- GREEN AVENTURINE is an excellent heart balancer and encourages easy expression of the emotions.

- AMAZONITE calms and balances the emotions and helps with throat and lung problems.

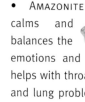

- MALACHITE helps dig out deep feelings and hurts, and can break unwanted ties and patterns of behaviour.

- MOSS AGATE is an ideal crystal for supporting the lungs and easing breathing difficulties, and feelings of being emotionally stifled.

- BLOODSTONE is a green quartz flecked with red jasper, giving it an active balance of energy and calm. It stimulates emotional growth while also aiding circulation of the blood.

- PERIDOT is a vivid light green crystal and a good cleanser of the subtle bodies, enabling us to initiate necessary change in our lives and encouraging personal growth.

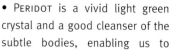

- EMERALD is a green type of the mineral beryl and is useful in guiding us to a personal direction for growth, bringing clarity to the heart and emotions.

The solar plexus chakra

The solar plexus chakra establishes us in our own sense of personal power. It is the power station of the body, physically related to the nervous, digestive and immune systems. The governing colour is yellow.

Major nerve centres are also found within the solar plexus. The ability to recognize and deal appropriately with energy of all kinds is the function of the solar plexus chakra. Information and control are the sources of all power. So an efficiently functioning solar plexus chakra imbues the individual with a sense of personal confidence, courage, optimism and ability to make the right decisions in any situation.

Since life in most modern societies is complex and demanding, as well as subject to many polluting influences, the solar plexus chakra can become overwhelmed and unbalanced. The result is an accumulation of stress and anxiety, the inability to resist infections, an intolerance to foods, additives and chemicals creating allergies, apathy and a loss of enthusiasm and humour. Mental clarity, memory and the ability to focus clearly and study will also be affected.

The solar plexus chakra and its related minor energy centres occupy the area below the ribcage and above the navel. Physically, this area of the body contains the digestive system enabling us to break down and assimilate nutrients from our food. Important organs such as the spleen are found here that sustain our immune system, protecting the body from dangerous micro-organisms in the outside world.

CRYSTALS FOR THE SOLAR PLEXUS CHAKRA

• AMBER is among the best-known of yellow crystals. Actually a pine resin, it varies in colour from pale yellow to a rich orange brown. It is beneficial for the nervous system and in self-healing processes.

▲ STRESS IS A WELL-KNOWN CAUSE OF MANY DIGESTIVE PROBLEMS. YELLOW STONES WILL HELP TENSE MUSCLES TO RELAX.

• RUTILATED QUARTZ is clear or smoky, and contains fine threads of golden or orange rutile crystals. It can move healing energy and works well with broken or damaged tissues.

• TIGER'S EYE is a yellow and brown banded form of shiny quartz, and is used to speed up energy flow and anchor subtle changes into the physical body.

• CITRINE QUARTZ can be bright and clear yellow in colour, and is used to keep the mind focused.

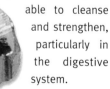

• IRON PYRITES, also known as "fool's gold" because of its yellow colour, is able to cleanse and strengthen, particularly in the digestive system.

The sacral chakra

The sacral chakra is located between the navel and the front of the pelvis, the pubic bones. Physically it is related to the reproductive organs and excretory systems. Orange stones naturally balance this chakra.

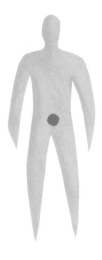

The energy of the sacral chakra focuses on sensation, feeling and movement. The exploration of the world and its pleasures and pains are the motivating energy of this centre. All types of creativity begin here. Flow is essential – the flow of curiosity, feelings and information, the fluid that feeds our cells and chemical processes, and the release of toxins from our system – all come under the influence of the sacral chakra. The sacral chakra, when balanced, encourages change and the moving to new adventures. Any form of restriction and rigidity can be helped with orange stones that will restore the natural qualities of the sacral chakra. Blocks of energy anywhere in the body can affect the physical organs and create problems. Infertility and impotence on any level can often be helped by releasing emotional blocks. Stiffness of joints, constipation,

▲ THE SACRAL CHAKRA IS THE WOMB OF ALL CREATIVITY AND THE BIRTH OF EVERY IDEA.

water retention and menstrual difficulties all originate from restricted energy flow. Likewise boredom, indifference or creative blocks indicate that the sacral chakra needs some attention.

CRYSTALS FOR THE SACRAL CHAKRA

• CARNELIAN is a popular orange crystal, and has a sense of warmth and gentle healing energy.

• ORANGE CALCITE offers delicate encouragement of potential, and with its soft and watery feel it can help melt away our problems.

• DARK CITRINE is a balanced and browny-orange stimulator and brings out practical creative skills, as well as being supporting and grounding.

• TOPAZ has elongated crystals and parallel striations, and is a clearing stone that will direct energy around the body.

• COPPER is used, in both nugget and in bracelet forms, to release any stagnation or a lack of flow in our physical and subtle body systems.

Other crystals used at the sacral chakra include ORANGE JASPER, TIGER'S EYE and SUNSTONE.

The base chakra

Esoterically, this first chakra is the red-coloured root of the lotus, whose thousand petals bloom at the crown. It is the basis and support of our complex physical, mental and subtle system, the source of our primal energy.

The base chakra is situated at the base of the spine and its main functions are to support consciousness within the physical body. All issues to do with survival and protection are focused at this point. The base chakra is concerned with practical skills, the reality of the present moment and the immediate needs of the individual. At a physical level the base chakra relates to all structural systems of

the body, especially the bones. Problems with physical movement, strained ligaments, pulled muscles and misaligned bones can be improved when the base chakra is balanced, as can be complaints affecting the colon, such as diarrhoea or constipation. Lack of

▲ KEEPING THE BODY'S ENERGIES MOVING FREELY AND EFFICIENTLY IS THE TASK OF THE BASE CHAKRA.

energy, fatigue and exhaustion, a loss of interest in life or an excessive interest in spirituality to the detriment of one's well-being, all indicate the need to enhance the life-energy of the base chakra through the use of red stones.

The base chakra is represented in Indian tradition by Ganesha, the elephant god, who guards a person's material wealth and good fortune. Ganesha is also venerated as overseeing the initiation of new projects or new directions in life, especially when taken on the basis of a secure material foundation.

Grounding, motivation and new starts are hence some of the keynotes of the body's first and base chakra. If the base chakra's energy is deep-rooted and strong, the entire chakra system rising from it can also be powerful and effective. It is a two-way conduit of energy in all its forms, both physical and subtle.

Crystals can be placed so that they rest on the ground between the legs, close to the base of the spine. Alternatively, stones can be placed on the top of the legs near to the groin area.

CRYSTALS FOR THE BASE CHAKRA

Among the stones often used at this chakra are:

• GARNET, in its red forms, is an efficient energizer. It can increase energy wherever it is placed and will also activate other stones placed nearby.

• JASPER is a reddish form of quartz, and helps to ground and gently activate the whole body when placed near to the base chakra.

• RUBY is a red variety of carborundum and combines well with energies of the heart centre as well as gently energizing the subtle bodies.

Brown and black crystals can also stabilize and balance the energies of the base chakra.

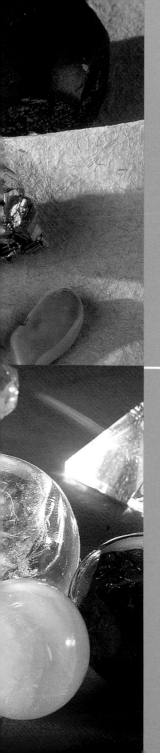

Crystal treatments

The therapeutic powers of crystals can be channelled to help balance bodily systems and emotions and to heal everyday complaints and ailments from headaches, migraine and menstrual cramps to stress, insomnia and lack of concentration. The following pages will advise you on how to select appropriate crystals to ease tension and calm the body and mind or boost energy levels. You will learn how to make gem essences so that you can benefit from a concentrated form of the stone's power. You will also discover how to enhance your surroundings by placing crystals in your home or work environment.

Relieving pain

Crystal healing is by its nature calming and relaxing. Painful conditions often seem to make the body tense itself. This can often prevent the proper flow of healing energy, blood, oxygen and nutrients to where they are needed.

The placement of crystals naturally begins to ease the imbalances that create pain. By releasing blockages within our subtle bodies, crystals can help stimulate the body's own healing mechanisms to work at a site of tension or pain.

BACKACHE RELIEF

Lodestone is an old name for magnetic iron ore, which was once used for navigational purposes. Placing one piece near the top of the neck and another at the base of the spine can help to relieve back tensions and stimulate spinal energies.

Help ease back pain with a small, clear quartz at the brow chakra. Imagine a beam of healing white light passing deep into your head with each in-breath.

CLEAR QUARTZ

▼ TO REALIGN THE BODY'S ENERGIES, USE EIGHT PIECES OF TOURMALINE. PLACE TWO AT THE CROWN, TWO MIDWAY ON EACH SIDE, AND TWO AT THE FEET. LIE DOWN AND REST INSIDE THIS CROSS-SHAPED ENERGY PATTERN.

EASING TENSE MUSCLES

Black or green tourmaline crystals (called also schorl and verdelite) have been found useful where structural adjustment is needed. Knotted muscles can be relieved by placing a piece near them. Neck, jaw or head tension can be eased by wearing earrings made of this stone.

▲ TURQUOISE CAN BE USED WHENEVER THERE IS A NEED FOR CALM, HEALING ENERGY.

▲ MALACHITE, A SOFT MINERAL FORM OF COPPER, IS GOOD AT CALMING PAINFUL AREAS AND DRAWING OUT IMBALANCES.

Malachite is a copper ore that forms in concentric bands of light and dark green. It can calm painful areas and draw out imbalances, but because it absorbs negativity it needs regular cleansing.

Copper can help to reduce inflammations

COPPER

and swellings, either in bracelet form or carried as a natural nugget in the pocket.

Turquoise can be placed on the body wherever there is pain, while carnelian is a powerful healer of the etheric body.

TURQUOISE

Among pink stones, rose quartz helps to calm aggravated areas and reduce the fears that accompany injury and pain. Placing pink stones at the solar plexus and sacral chakras can help to soothe both mind and body.

ROSE QUARTZ

Soothing headaches

Headaches tend to occur when there is an imbalance or blockage of energy to the head. Amethyst, with its long tradition as an effective healing stone, can be very useful in soothing headaches.

All cool-coloured stones (blue, indigo and violet) are useful where there is an energy imbalance resulting in restriction of energy flow and experience of pain. Headaches are notoriously individual in cause and cure. Amethyst, combining the colours of red and blue, is a good crystal to try as it naturally tends to bring balance in any extreme situation.

HEADACHE RELIEF

If a headache can be caught in its early stages it can be a lot easier to reduce the symptoms with crystal healing. First of all, try a simple chakra layout using the appropriate colour stone at each chakra. This will help to stabilize all energy levels in the body.

▼ AMETHYST IS AN ESSENTIAL PART OF YOUR HEALING CRYSTAL COLLECTION.

HEAD-SOOTHING CRYSTAL LAYOUT

Place one amethyst point on either side of the base of the neck, just above the collar bones, pointing upwards. Place a third stone, also pointing upwards, on the centre of the forehead. A fourth may be added if desired at the top of the head. This placing brings the throat, brow and crown chakras into powerful harmony.

Another common cause of headaches is an imbalance between the head energy and that at the solar plexus, often the result of stress or unsuitable food. If you have a headache and an upset stomach, for example, use a stone that will also balance the solar plexus, such as ametrine.

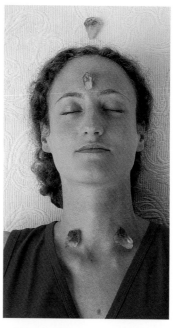

▲ A FOUR-STONE AMETHYST LAYOUT TO SOOTHE HEADACHES.

▶ GENTLY MASSAGING UP THE LINE OF THE JAW, ACROSS THE FOREHEAD AND SKULL AND PARTICULARLY THE BASE OF THE SKULL WITH A SMOOTH POLISHED QUARTZ CRYSTAL CAN HELP TO REDUCE TENSION AND PAIN.

Easing PMS and menstrual cramps

Period pains and menstrual cramps are often made worse by physical and emotional tensions, which restrict the body's natural energy flows. Moonstones and opal are among the stones recommended for easing these tensions.

CALMING THE EMOTIONS

Moonstone helps in balancing and relaxing emotional states, and also works beneficially on all fluid systems of the body, relieving pain in the abdominal area. Traditional Ayurvedic texts in India state that moonstone is the ideal stone for women to wear, and indeed, it can be made into charming jewellery.

MOONSTONES

RELIEVING STOMACH CRAMPS

Dark opal is similar in properties to moonstone, acting powerfully at the first and second chakras to ease menstrual cramps in a short time. Place a small piece in a hip or trouser pocket.

DARK OPALS

To reinforce chakra healing for PMS, carry with you a dark opal or an orange stone, such as carnelian, associated with the sacral chakra. When you have the chance, rub the stone lightly across your lower abdomen, from just below the navel, making a large circle to the left, and allowing it to spiral towards the middle. Feel the warmth of the crystal's energy flowing into you from the stone and the easing of tension that this brings.

CARNELIAN

FIVE-MOONSTONE PATTERN

A healing pattern of five moonstones amplifies the relaxing and therapeutic potential of the stone to ease physical and emotional tensions. Lying down comfortably, position one stone at the top of your head, one near each armpit and one on each hip.

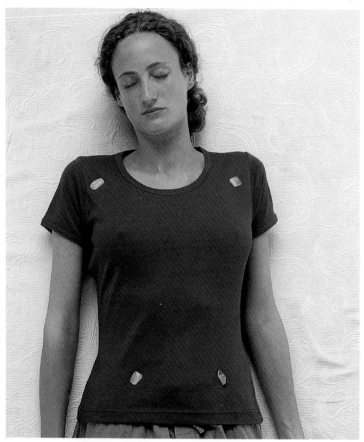

▲ FIND A COMFORTABLE POSITION IN WHICH TO LIE DOWN, CLOSE YOUR EYES AND ALLOW THE FIVE-MOONSTONE PATTERN TO EASE AWAY ANY MENSTRUAL TENSIONS WITHIN YOUR BODY.

Energizing crystals

Sometimes poor energy is simply caused by a temporary imbalance in the chakra system, especially the base and solar plexus. Redistribution of natural energy reserves can help to revitalize depleted areas, and restore vitality.

▲ FOR A QUICK ENERGY BOOST TO THE WHOLE SYSTEM, HOLD A CLEAR QUARTZ CRYSTAL, POINT UPWARDS, IN EACH HAND, AND PLACE A LARGE CITRINE STQNE AT THE SOLAR PLEXUS.

Red, orange and yellow stones, such as garnet, amber and topaz, can promote increased energy. Yellow citrine makes a wonderful substitute for summer sun on a dull winter's day.

More earthy tones, such as tiger's eye, dark citrine and jasper, can help you focus on practical action to be taken.

GARNET

AMBER

TOPAZ

JASPER

CITRINE

TIGER'S EYE

DARK CITRINE

Aiding concentration

The natural, organized structure of a crystal lattice automatically increases the clarity and orderliness of a study area or workplace. A beautiful clear crystal such as quartz can bring stillness and focus to the mind.

Yellow is known to stimulate the logical functions of the mind, so a bright yellow amber, citrine or fluorite will assist your memory and recall. Fluorite is particularly good as it helps balance the working of the brain hemispheres.

Deep blue stones, such as kyanite, sodalite and sapphire, will encourage your communication skills and a better understanding of ideas and concepts.

CITRINE

FLUORITE

▲ KEEP A FAVOURITE CRYSTAL NEAR YOU AS YOU STUDY, AND TAKE IT WITH YOU TO AN EXAM FOR EXTRA CONFIDENCE AND CLARITY.

SODALITE

KYANITE

AMBER

SAPPHIRE

Releasing stress

A shock, accident or loss may leave you shaken and vulnerable. Look out for stress symptoms, such as tensing of muscles, recurrent mental replays of events and sudden welling up of emotions.

CALMING LAYOUT

The effects of stress can be released by this layout. Continue regularly until the stress eases.

1 Place a rose quartz at the heart chakra, with four quartz points facing outwards, positioned diagonally around it.

2 At the sacral chakra, below the navel, place a tiger's eye, and surround it with another four quartz points, facing inwards and also placed diagonally around it.

3 The stones at the heart release emotional tension, while those on the abdomen balance the chakras above and give grounded energy and stability.

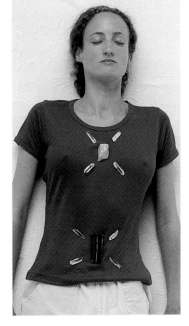

▲ YOU WILL NEED EIGHT SMALL, CLEAR QUARTZ CRYSTALS, A ROSE QUARTZ AND A TIGER'S EYE.

CLEAR QUARTZ

ROSE QUARTZ

TIGER'S EYE

Calming crystals

Here is a calming crystal layout to help during times of emotional stress to restore calm and equilibrium. Signs of stress being released include muscle twitches, deep breaths or sighs, yawning and watery eyes.

SOOTHING CRYSTAL LAYOUT

1 Place a rose quartz at the heart chakra, surrounded by four quartz points in a cross formation. Points should be facing outwards to remove emotional imbalances; or set points facing inwards to stabilize an over-emotional state.

2 Position a citrine stone at the solar plexus chakra, with its darker point facing downwards. This increases the sense of security and feeling of safety.

3 Place an amethyst on the third eye chakra to calm the mind. If the release is found to be too strong, remove stones from the heart area and place a hand over the solar plexus.

▲ FOR A CALMING LAYOUT USE FOUR CLEAR QUARTZ CRYSTALS, A ROSE QUARTZ, A CITRINE AND AN AMETHYST.

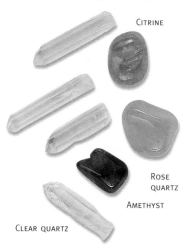

CITRINE

ROSE QUARTZ

AMETHYST

CLEAR QUARTZ

Aiding restful sleep

Taking crystals to bed is an easy and comforting way of dealing with insomnia. Experiment with different crystals for different types of sleeplessness. Hold the stones, put them on or under your pillow or near to you as you settle.

DEALING WITH SLEEPLESS NIGHTS
Chrysoprase, an apple green form of chalcedony quartz, has been found in many cases to encourage peaceful sleep. Place a stone under your pillow or by your bedside table.

If tension or worry is the cause of restlessness, try amethyst, rose quartz or citrine.

If something you have eaten is disturbing your sleep pattern, a digestive calmer such as ametrine, moonstone or iron pyrites may work for you.

CHRYSOPRASE

AMETHYST

CITRINE

ROSE QUARTZ

IRON PYRITES

AMETRINE

▲ HOLD THE APPROPRIATE STONES OR HAVE THEM NEARBY AS YOU SLEEP.

Banishing bad dreams

Where there is fear, particularly related to bad dreams, place a grounding and protecting stone, such as tourmaline, staurolite or smoky quartz at the bottom of the bed. Labradorite can also help chase away unwelcome thoughts or feelings.

A stronger energy might be needed to counter nightmares: place a large, smooth moss agate or tektite by the bed where you can touch it and feel its reassuring solidity.

STAUROLITE

TOURMALINE

SMOKY QUARTZ

MOSS AGATE

▼ IF TENSION AND WORRY ARE THE CAUSES OF RESTLESSNESS TRY PLACING ROSE QUARTZ, AMETHYST OR CITRINE BY YOUR PILLOW.

Crystal essences

You can benefit from the healing properties of gems by making your own crystal essences. These are vibrational preparations made by immersing gemstones in spring water and exposing to direct sunlight.

Gem essences are believed to work by allowing the energy pattern of a chosen stone to be imprinted on the water. Sunlight is best for this process, but leaving a stone in water by your bedside overnight and drinking the water first thing in the morning can also be beneficial. Remove the stone before using the essence.

The charged water can be drunk on the spot or bottled for later use in helping the healing processes of the body. It is not necessary to ingest a gem essence in order for it to be effective.

Rubbing a few drops on pulse points or around a chakra area, or close to an area of imbalance can work just as well. Keep crystal essence bottles in the fridge and try to drink them within one week. You should not freeze them. Fresh-made essence is usually best. You can also spray indoor plants or add the essence water to your bath.

Caution: some stones are toxic or dissolve in water (crystals of salt, for example). Gem water made from the quartz family is safe. Try citrine, amethyst or tiger's eye.

◀ DRINKING A HOME-MADE CRYSTAL ESSENCE, SUCH AS THIS ONE MADE BY PLACING AN AMETHYST IN CLEAR SPRING WATER, GIVES YOU A CONCENTRATED FORM OF YOUR STONE'S HEALING POWER.

MAKING A MOONSTONE ESSENCE

A moonstone essence has the ability to calm our emotions. Moonstone is soft and cooling, because of its feminine orientation.

1 Take a cleansed gemstone and place it into a clear glass bowl. Fill the bowl with fresh spring water until the stone is covered.

2 Leave the bowl outside under the light of a full moon for three hours, or overnight if the night is calm and clear.

3 Remove the moonstone, remembering to cleanse it after use, and pour the liquid into a clear glass.

4 Take a drink of the moonstone infusion first thing in the morning in order to prepare yourself for a harmonious day.

Enhancing your home

Crystals can make attractive decorations for the home and they can also enhance the surroundings by bringing a balancing and cleansing influence on many levels, helping to neutralize emotional debris and pollution.

▲ ADDING CRYSTALS TO A SACRED SPACE KEEPS THE ENERGIES FRESH AND POSITIVE.

Crystals can create a sacred space in your home, as a simple quiet place in which to rest or as an elaborate altar with sacred images. Honour an anniversary or guest with a temporary special space or set aside a permanent meditative area in your home or garden.

Make a crystal lightbox by placing a large transparent or translucent stone in front of a light source. Change the mood by using a yellow crystal for relaxation, red for energy and violet for mystery.

▶ CRYSTALS WITH INTERNAL FRACTURES OR RAINBOWS, SUCH AS RUTILATED QUARTZ OR MOSS AGATE, CAN MAKE BEAUTIFUL LIGHTS.

◀ CRYSTALS IN AN AQUARIUM REVEAL THEIR VIVID COLOURS, AND ALSO ENERGIZE THE SURROUNDINGS.

▲ CREATE A MINI ZEN GARDEN BY FILLING A FLAT BOWL WITH CLEAN SAND OR DRY GRAVEL. ARRANGE INTERESTING STONES AND CRYSTALS ON IT, AND USE A COMB OR FORK TO DRAW PATTERNS IN THE SAND.

Pets can be treated with gems and crystals, both to maintain health and when they are unwell. Use a crystal pendulum to balance the energy in four-footed animals, or place crystals safely around a sleeping area. Energizing water can be dropped on your fingers and then stroked through the fur of a cat or dog. A small gemstone can be attached to a dog or cat collar. Sick animals may find the presence of a crystal in their basket or hutch comforting.

A quiet corner of the garden is a good place for reflection, and crystals placed near the plants keep them healthy too. House plants benefit from crystals placed in their soil, quartz and emerald (gem quality is not necessary) are popular. Aquamarine and jade are also said to enhance plant energies, while turquoise can help plants recover from damage and disease.

▲ A QUARTZ CRYSTAL WILL ENHANCE A HOUSE PLANT'S OVERALL HEALTH.

enhancing your home **59**

Crystals in the workplace

Whether you work at home or in the office, crystals can be used to enhance your working area in simple, effective ways. Consider the factors you would most like to improve and select the types of colour and crystal that might help.

If you work in an office or factory, there is much you can do to make your personal space a pleasing place to be:

• Keep natural stones or crystals as paperweights or as dividers in a file or bookcase.

• Use carved stone pots or bowls on the desk as containers in which to store pens or paperclips.

• Place stones on the soil of potted plants in your work area.

• Have a favourite crystal as a "worry stone" for your pocket.

The telephone and computer can be particular causes of tension and stress, demanding our attention and raising the body's adrenaline levels when emotions are triggered.

▶ KEEP A SMALL BOWL OF STONES NEAR THE PHONE AS A FOCUS FOR YOUR ATTENTION. IT WILL ALSO HELP AVOID UNNECESSARY DEPLETION OF YOUR ENERGY BY BECOMING OVERLY INVOLVED IN OTHER PEOPLE'S PROBLEMS.

▲ OFFSET THE STRONG ELECTROMAGNETIC FIELDS CREATED BY COMPUTER SCREENS BY PUTTING A CRYSTAL ON THE MONITOR OR NEAR IT. CLEAR QUARTZ IS RECOMMENDED, BUT IT MUST BE CLEANSED FREQUENTLY.

Moonstone helps to foster understanding of our colleagues' points of view and, as such, is an excellent aid to communication. It also acts to balance our emotional states and clear away tensions, and restores the balance of the body's fluid systems.

SNOWFLAKE OBSIDIAN

Obsidian is a form of black volcanic glass, often with white flecks (snowflake obsidian), patches of dark red (mahogany obsidian) or a smoky translucence (Apache tears). It is known as a good aid to concentration, working patiently to bring imbalances to the surface and reveal hidden factors surrounding a situation. Other stones can then assist by clearing away this clutter, leaving the mind clear and focused.

Fluorite is also found in a variety of colours, with violet or mauve among the most frequent. Its presence can help in a work environment through its capacity to release dynamic or inspirational ideas, as it is associated with the crown chakra and acts as a link between subtle and practical aspects of consciousness. FLUORITE

crystals in the workplace **61**

Crystal colours directory

 We have seen how coloured crystals are associated with the chakra system, and how they work in many different types of healing. This directory looks briefly at the most commonly used crystals according to their colours.

DIRECTORY OF COLOURED CRYSTALS

Note that some crystals are listed below under several colours. The colour categories are rarely exact in practice, and good stones can be a little or widely different from the suggested match.

This variety and individuality, however, is part of the attraction of choosing crystals. Finding a stone that resonates to your own vibration is the beginning of your healing experience.

RED	garnet, jasper, ruby, red tiger's eye, carnelian.
ORANGE	carnelian, orange calcite, dark citrine, topaz, copper, sunstone.
YELLOW	amber, rutilated quartz, tiger's eye, citrine quartz, iron pyrites, yellow topaz.
GREEN	green aventurine, malachite, bloodstone, amazonite, moss agate, peridot, emerald, jade.
BLUE	aquamarine, turquoise, blue lace agate, celestite, sapphire, sodalite.
INDIGO	lapis lazuli, sodalite, kyanite, azurite, sapphire.
VIOLET	amethyst, fluorite, sugilite, iolite, kunzite, charoite.
WHITE	clear quartz, herkimer diamond, Iceland spa, moonstone, selenite.
BLACK	smoky quartz, obsidian, tourmaline, haematite.
PINK	rose quartz, rhodonite, kunzite, rhodocrosite.
MULTICOLOURED	opal, azurite-malachite, labradorite, hawk's eye, ametrine.

Quartz: the family that has everything

There is one remarkable family of crystals that on its own encompasses most of the colours and healing opportunities of the spectrum. As such, it deserves a special mention in any study of crystals.

QUARTZ is probably one of the commonest minerals on Earth, being composed of the abundant elements silica and oxygen. Stones in the quartz family may be bright, clear and simple or dark, dense and complex, depending on the heat and pressure involved in their formation. Colours and forms vary widely because the crystal lattice allows other atoms to enter at a microscopic level. These often alter the way that light passes through them, changing the visible colour.

CLEAR QUARTZ is colourless and shiny; MILKY QUARTZ is white, as is OPAL (the high water content creating a display of flashing colour); ROSE QUARTZ is pink and translucent, while CARNELIAN is orange and JASPER is often red, but also yellow, green and blue; RUTILATED QUARTZ is golden yellow and CITRINE ranges from yellow to orange-brown; CHRYSOPRASE is bright apple-green and AVENTURINE is green or blue, with tiny sparks of mica or pyrites; in the blue range are the delicate BLUE LACE AGATE

and dreamy purple AMETHYST; among the mixed colours are the agates, with wavy parallel coloured bands, including MOSS AGATE and BANDED AGATE, and TIGER'S EYE, with subtle browns, yellows, blue and red; at the darkest end of the spectrum are SMOKY QUARTZ, BLOODSTONE, or HELIOTROPE, in a dark, shiny green, TOURMALINE QUARTZ, embedded with fine black needles and onyx, with its straight lines of white on black.

index